The American Dream Journey

The American Dream Journey

Feliciano Marroquín Orantes

www.librosenred.com

Dirección General: Marcelo Perazolo
Dirección de Contenidos: Ivana Basset
Diseño de cubierta: Daniela Ferrán
Diagramación de interiores: Virginia Ruano

Está prohibida la reproducción total o parcial de este libro, su tratamiento informático, la transmisión de cualquier forma o de cualquier medio, ya sea electrónico, mecánico, por fotocopia, registro u otros métodos, sin el permiso previo escrito de los titulares del Copyright.

Primera edición en español - Impresión bajo demanda

© LibrosEnRed, 2008
Una marca registrada de Amertown International S.A.

ISBN: 978-1-59754-342-2

Para encargar más copias de este libro o conocer otros libros de esta colección visite www.librosenred.com

Dedication

This book is to my parents, siblings, nephews and nieces. I dedicate it also to my teachers, friends and other people who illuminated my way and filled it with life, wisdom, love and good moments. This is for all of them, because they contributed their grain of sand for me to become the person I now am.

I want to specially acknowledge my teacher Otto Noe Ruano, Mr. Arcenio Castillo Colindres, Everardo Lozano and Darrell Lee; this book would have not been possible without you.

Feliciano Marroquín

Prologue

Illegal immigration has existed in different countries for thousands of years. It can be said that from the beginning of history, there have been people fleeing persecution because of their religious or political beliefs, their family situation, and even because of their skin color. Today, people move more commonly due to economic problems, and they go especially to the United States of America.

It is said that if you arrive there, all your economic problems will disappear and you will have everything you have ever imagined. This dazzles many young minds, from countrymen to university students, who leave behind their present lives, their families, schools and careers to fetch the "American dream". Blinded by their desire to get there, they forget their most valuable possession; their life.

Reaching such a dream becomes a priority over everything else, and they cannot imagine what the future may bring. The survivor's pitfalls along the way are put aside and become isolated or secret, because of feelings of shame. We only tell our successes, and doing that, we attract more aspirants to jump onto this train, contributing to the well-known "calling effect".

Therefore, I praise the effort of my friend Feliciano Marroquín Orantes who reaffirms his solidarity towards our American countries and rescues –for our enjoyment and enlightenment and as a legacy for future generations– a magnificent collection of true events experienced in his own flesh, opening the door to allow us to witness his trip through his own eyes.

He offers us his wonderful book: American dream journey whose varied content will enrich us and move us to reflection.

I am convinced that the many readers of this work will find it an orienting lighthouse as they consider embarking upon the unpredictable adventure of the American dream journey.

As well as aiding us to understand and appreciate the effort of those willing to risk their lives to bring bread to their children's mouth.

Everardo Lozano Lemus

Origins of the story

The American Dream Journey is not a fictional story or a novel; it is the true adventure of a group of illegal immigrants and their heroic deeds to enter the United States.

Originally, what you are reading was written as a personal diary by one of the adventurers called Tito, who recorded these events, lived during the three-month trip towards the land everybody talks about. He decided to publish it years later, after friends and family convinced him to do so due to the exciting content of it.

Tito was a 17-year-old young man from Guatemala, belonging to a family of nine children. He showed very early his enthusiasm of making it big by re-selling bread, lemons, bananas, and even wild flowers to nearby rural communities since he was 8 years old. At the young age of seventeen, he had finished the second-to-the-last year of an accounting degree, while working as an elementary teacher and in the literacy campaign for adults in the afternoons. School was out during the coffee harvesting season in December and January every year allowing Tito to earn extra income ($2.50 a day) picking coffee in the coffee fields.

Before registering for the last year of his degree, he found out how much he would earn as an accountant in Guatemala. He felt deceived, because he was dreaming of something better that would allow him to help his parents and siblings.

With that in mind, and having heard the stories of people who succeeded in the North, arrangements for his departure were made. That is the origin of *The American Dream Journey.*

Everardo Lozano Lemus

The Farewell

There is not always happiness in life. Sometimes we are forced to say goodbye; all the pronounced words do not sooth the pain of knowing that perhaps it is the last time you will see the people you love.

I could have a future here if I want, but I don't see myself pursuing it this way because I have been cursed with the free spirit of a dreamer that leads me inevitably towards adventures, to seek something better. I know that I move stubbornly towards the unknown, with my heart full of hopes and dreams.

Today, January 24th, after getting up at four in the morning to start this so-longed-for trip, my mother is looking at me with eyes of sadness. She seems to be trying to say something, while she prepares my backpack and I drink that which may be the last cup of coffee prepared by my mom's wonderful hands. My mother filled my school backpack with black plastic, aspirins, bicarbonate, one shirt, one pair of pants, a ski hat, wool gloves and a coat.

Yesterday I said farewell to my friends; I can't forget the school, the exchange with classmates, and those unending afternoons when we ran around, under the rain, doing homework. I can't forget the town dogs and the flavored *tostadas* the lunch lady sold at the park where we mingled every afternoon.

While enjoying my cup of coffee, I remembered the goodbye of my sisters. They wished me luck, gave me lots of advise and their blessing.

Among grins, sobs and strong hugs, I said goodbye to my mother and grandmother, with a lump in my throat and tears betraying my effort for not crying. I got on the old Land Rover, with its paint coming off, that we treasured so much since it served the family well in all circumstances.

My father, Mr. Marroquín, and my sister Mary came with me for the beginning of the trip. In route to Barberena, Santa Rosa, where I was going to be picked up by the coyote, we could feel the tension in the car, they looked at me with sadness and with the traditional grin that pretends to be a smile, while I was looking through the window at the cane and coffee fields, the bus stops, the acquaintances waving as we went by, and even a green iguana that was there sunbathing each time I traveled that road. I knew that I was leaving my childhood, filled with good memories, in that place; my homeland.

Sighs went and came until we arrived to Barberena, around eight in the morning. We parked and waited for the white suburban that was coming to take me away. While waiting, we passed the time pretending that nothing was happening, chatting about a million irrelevant things, trying to forget that which was about to unfold. At the same time, I was looking at the trucks, pedestrians, lunch ladies and ice cream men that were running by fighting to get on the urban buses to sell their goods.

Around two thirty in the afternoon, a coyote's assistant appeared driving a white suburban.

Leaving the nest

With a strange mix of happiness and grief, I received my father's and sister's hugs. They wished me good luck and gave me good advice.

I felt like an eagle leaving the nest, with my wings spread against the wind, with the hope and the illusion of flying very high, as I went away and turned to see my loved ones and thought "thank you, I will come back and reward you".

We started the trip to the capital city of Guatemala, where I would meet the other victims of a very long journey.

The guys who drove the old, run down suburban, did not seem trustworthy to me; they looked like crooks and drug dealers. The suburban stalled out both at Puerta Parada and El Trébol and we had to get off and push.

Struggling and wishing not to have any more car problems, we arrived to a car dealer's office, where the coyote gathered the people before departure. There I met whom we later called Ñoño and Mrs. Rosa; they were also traveling. Mrs. Rosa was a forty-five-year-old lady from El Salvador, short, very kind and smiley. On the other hand, Ñoño was a very serious and reserved man from San Marcos, Guatemala, with dark skin and deep eyes.

That same night I gave six thousand five hundred *quetzals* to the coyote's helpers (1,000 USD) the fee I had to pay in Guatemala. I got the money from my older brothers, Arnoldo and Samuel. I had left in my pocket one thousand quetzals (150 USD) for my own expenses; I had earned the money working in the coffee fields in the summer of 1996. I kept that hidden in a little bag that my mom had sewn to my underwear to prevent a possible theft.

The following day, while I was watching a soccer match being played in the backyard of the car dealer, two people appeared. I had seen them before; they lived in villages close to mine and I had known them all my life. Byron, a young man, about nineteen years old, short and fair skinned and Mrs. María; a thirty-two-year-old widow whose husband had recently been murdered and mother of 3 little girls under 10 years old, who lived by the gravel road I used to follow everyday for two hours when I was working as a teacher in 1996.

I felt such joy from seeing them; we had never spoken before, although we exchanged occasional hellos and goodbyes. However, at that moment, we felt that we knew each other personally, and we greeted as if we were old friends, smiling and surprised to find out that we were going to travel together. We talked all the way back to the car dealer's place. There we found all the people that were going to travel with us.

The Instructions

After being introduced, the coyote –a tall man, bold, muscular, well dressed, with gold on his teeth, thick neck chains and rings on almost all his fingers–, began giving us instructions: "Never mention who the coyote is; if Mexican authorities ask you, you tell them that you are traveling alone, that you came from different places and met on the way, that you know nothing of each other and that you have just met traveling on the same road. Try not to talk too much; in other words, try not to talk at all in front of the Mexicans, because they'll notice your Central American accents and deport you back here. The clocks' alarms need to be silenced or turned off. Something very important: we are traveling together; therefore, we have to help each other if we want to arrive safely. I won't drive you personally, but I will escort you by traveling on legal Mexican territory to deliver food and supplies, as you need them. The men should respect the women that wish to be respected; the ones that don't want to be respected are on their own. I can't deny that it gets cold during the trip; you are all adults and I am not your father to tell you what you should do".

"We'll leave today at 11:00 AM for the Mexican border. We'll travel by bus and we'll stop and spend the night in a small town called Camojá, in Huehuetenango, which is on this side of the Mexican border."

Unknown roads

Grouped in pairs, we waited for the bus to Huehuetenango with high hopes; in the meantime, we tried to become acquainted and asked each other questions such as "Where are you from?" or "Who is waiting for you in the US?".

When I climbed on to the bus, I realized that I was beginning to travel unknown roads, perhaps for the first and last time. I was gradually leaving Guatemala behind, its serene mountains and volcanoes. The noise of the bus in the background was sometimes interrupted by the assistant yelling to people on the road "Come on, Get on, there're still empty spots!".

While filling my mind with the beautiful Guatemalan images of the landscape and buildings I noticed that Norma, a young woman –about twenty three years old– from the state of Petén did not find a place to sit and was traveling standing. Immediately I stood up to yield her my seat. She accepted it with no hesitation, smiling and thanking me for my gentleman's attitude. Little did I know at the time that my gesture would be the beginning of a wonderful friendship; we started talking about school and even shared some jokes. After a while, she asked me if I was tired of traveling standing up, and offered me to sit on her lap. I had no time to reply.

I wanted to refuse –I felt embarrassed–, but the other guys looked at me with admiration and started saying "You lucky toothpick!" and laughed. By then, they had already given me the nickname "toothpick" for being the smaller and thinner one in the group. I wanted to sit on her lap, of course, but I was shy. Then, without giving it another thought, I reacted decisively; sat on her lap and thanked her. She placed one arm around my waist and we kept talking peacefully, although I felt a bit nervous.

Everybody talked about many things during the trip. Mrs. María talked about her daughters, Mrs. Rosa about her sons, and both about the things they were going to do with the money they would earn in the United States; the guys talked about meeting North American girls and having a good time with them. Everybody believed and trusted that we were going to get there safely.

Time went by quickly, sharing our dreams and hopes, arriving to the state of Huehuetenango at six in the afternoon. We waited there about twenty minutes for the arrival of the following bus that was taking us to Camojá. We made it to Camojá very tired, around nine at night where we could rest until the following day when we were going to attempt crossing the Mexican-Guatemalan border.

The Hotel

Once in Camojá, we walked for ten minutes to reach the hotel called "El Pobre Simón", located a mile and a half away from La Mesilla; the Mexican border.

This was our second night away from home, one of many that we spent ignoring our future. We slept on old pads, furnished with a pair of sheets. To minimize hotel expenses, all the men shared one room and all the women another, sleeping on the concrete floor.

The following dawn, the crowing of roosters and the noise of cars going by in front of the hotel woke us up. We greeted each other good morning and with sleepy faces and dragon breath, we asked the guides: "When are we leaving? At what time?" They did not give us a clear answer; they said, "Probably today in the afternoon, but we are not sure."

As a pastime, Norma, María, Ulises and I went to walk around the town market. Ulises was a young man, approximately twenty four years old, from the capital city; he was going to reunite with his mother in the United States. It was evident that he was a city person for his way of dressing and talking. He was a really cool guy.

While walking around the market, many people approached us offering to exchange Guatemalan money for Mexican currency. We had been warned not to do so, unless we were all together, because we could get robbed. The guides were going to tell us when and where we could exchange it. After wandering for a while and eating a corn on the cob, we went back to the hotel; there we received the bad news that we were not going to leave that day.

The next day found us in the same uncertain situation, with a big question mark in our foreheads. We were asking the same question: "When are we leaving?" receiving the same answer all over again; not even the guides had a certain idea of what was going to happen. Like the day before, I went for a walk moved by my curiosity to know Mexico. Towards the border, I met three fellow travelers: María, Rosa and Norma. They were watching the river running under a bridge over the road. We decided to go down to the river where we talked for a while and threw rocks to the curious fish that were sticking their heads out of the water to observe us. We spent a long time there and then returned to the hotel. At night, we were informed that we were leaving the following day. We felt better and could sleep with the happy thought that we were going to continue forward with our journey.

The morning of the third day was different. We knew we were going to try crossing the border, and to get our bodies ready for it, Ulises, Byron, Mike and I decided to play some basketball in a nearby court I had spotted the day I went to the market. Mike was also from the capital city; he was short, talkative, with dark skin and about twenty years of age. His uncle, who was living in the United States, helped him to pay for the trip.

We bought a plastic ball and ran around the court for a while. The actual game was short because we were worried about the trip. We returned to the hotel to find everybody with disappointed and upset faces; crossing was difficult and not even the guides knew when we were going to leave. At that moment, most of us got angry; some started complaining about being stuck in that place, unable to do anything and eating beans and eggs every day, morning and afternoon.

Threatened with shotguns

Five days went by without knowing anything about the crossing, until, finally, one day without previous notice, three 4x4 Toyota pickup trucks arrived and the guide yelled: "Let's go! Quick, get into the trucks parked outside and let's go! Come on, hurry up!" sharing smiles of joy we packed our few things in a rush, and ran smiling towards the trucks. We got on one of them, because the other two were already loaded with a group of about fifty individuals from El Salvador, Honduras, and Peru led by other guides. We formed a patchwork of different cultures and beliefs with a common goal: to arrive on the other side of the border.

To avoid crossing directly through the entry port to Mexico, they took us on dirt roads, going around the border. Poor people in the cars behind the first one that was leaving clouds of dust as it advanced! The road was full of holes and stones; sometimes the dirt became mud. After a while, we could make out some white towers in the distance that resembled pieces of candy at the top of the mountains which marked the dividing line between Guatemala and Mexico.

While moving ahead, some tall cowboys intercepted us by blocking the road pointing shotguns at us. We all felt scared and were ready to give them all we had. I remembered then my shrewd mother that had sewn the little bag on to my underwear. Calmly, I thought of giving them everything except that hidden in a secret place. My only fear was to be killed there, in the middle of nowhere.

Luckily, the men turned out to be the owners of the land whose private roads we were trespassing. The guides had to give them money for them to allow us to go through. When they realized we were illegal, they accepted a generous gift from the guide and allowed us to continue. They even gave us directions.

Once, we got lost in a place where the road turned into a dead end. We had to go back and ask some locals who lived in small houses made out of wooden sticks, in the middle of the forest. On that kind of road, you get very tired of riding six hours standing up with the shaking of the truck. At six in the afternoon we reached a ravine, at the edge of which amazingly, people were selling clothing, food, hats and even exchanging quetzals for pesos, since we were only a step away from the border between Guatemala and Mexico.

There we were instructed to exchange our money, and for the first time I had in my hands Mexican currency. To be honest, it made me smile, because it seemed to be play money, like the one we used to play grocery store with when we were little. There we bought food and all that we needed.

We got off the trucks and began walking, following the guides towards a nearby village under the name of Gracias a Dios (Thanks to God). It was certainly an adequate name; after such a long trip, the only thing that came to our minds was to thank God for stopping the tiring ride in the trucks, even when we had not arrived yet to our destination.

A HORRIFYING EXPERIENCE

Everything started when we approached the village of Gracias a Dios. At the entrance, there was a barefoot man, with a machete on his waist, disheveled, with only one tooth, and dressed in rags. He got in our way and threatened not to let us through the village unless we paid an entrance fee. One of the guides took care of his plea and we continued ahead.

From the distance, the place seemed a nice rural town where children ran barefooted surrounded by chickens and puppies on dirt patios. However, as we got closer, the village seemed to be one taken from a horror movie in which the protagonist arrives to a deserted town where nothing is heard but the wind whistling in the dark. The town was all silence; in one half-torn-down house the door creaked when moved by the wind, once and again. There wasn't a single person anywhere, although we were walking among houses. We were aware of the tension in the air and turned around constantly while following the guides who seem to be walking by leaps and bounds.

Finally, we arrived to a very small house, like the dwarfs' home in Snow White. The guys called it "el panteoncito" (the niche) because it was so tiny. We settled in the best we could and, as if it were prearranged, immediately the guides announced that it was time to eat. They started serving the first course that already had a Mexican flavor; we weren't used to eating hot food and we felt that it wasn't a meal with chili, but mainly chili. Nevertheless, since we hadn't eaten all day, we finished our servings sweating and sighing. It was curious that the guides were providing everything and didn't let us leave the house at all, not to raise any suspicion according to them. We could only go to the backyard of the house to urinate, and we didn't see a single person, not even the cook that prepared our meal.

Crossing the Mexican border

The following day, before the crack of dawn and the crowing of roosters, we heard a cry: "Everybody up! Let's go!" It was four in the morning. Aware of the place and having slept with our clothes on, we knew that drinking a good cup of morning coffee or brushing our teeth weren't possible options, so we got up, rubbed our eyes, put on our backpacks and started walking uphill through narrow, stony paths. It was dark and you could barely see the person in front of you. Luckily, I had bought a small flashlight in the Camojá market that illuminated the way for me and several of my companions, although a couple people fell and hurt their knees.

After walking for three hours, with the first light of the morning, the fog settled at the top of the mountain and the guides decided to stop and rest. Despite having walked for three hours, we still felt very cold; the morning dew, the fog and the sweat felt like a splash of cold water on our backs, and we preferred to keep walking. Moving ahead among trees, bushes, muddy roads and thick vegetation, the day surprised us while crossing the dividing line. We finally set foot onto Mexican soil.

Once in Mexico, we felt accomplished; we were still doing well and we had come a long way. In Guatemala, our families did not know anything about us; my family later told me that the coyote never answered their phone calls. They waited in despair for any news.

At ten in the morning, while walking on Mexican land, we approached a village with houses made out of pine bark; we could see about six or seven small houses with Century plant roofs that seemed inhabited; smoke came out of all of them indicating that somebody was there but we did not see anyone.

Going through the village, we arrived to a small house with similar characteristics to the one described above, but this one was actually a little store that sold basic goods. We bought several things from an old lady who kept calling us "sons". Suddenly a man approached us, looked at us from head to toe, and asked us what we were doing there. His attitude changed when he realized that we were on the American Dream Journey. He started talking to us in a different tone and confessed that he was from Honduras and had spent three months in that village unable to cross to the other side. He advised us not to cross, because we were going to be caught.

Ignoring the man's advice, we rested for a while and resumed walking, after saying good-bye to the sweet old lady and the Honduran brother.

We walked for about an hour, crossing forests and wire fences, and finally arrived to the place where a truck was going to pick us up, under some pine trees on a dirt road. We laid down on the dried, fallen pine tree leaves that served us as a comfortable, soft bed. The blue sky, the cool breeze and wind whistling in the pine trees were very relaxing.

After a while, there was only silence; only the birds singing, perhaps announcing a storm, could be heard, while we rested peacefully and waited for our transportation.

At two o'clock in the afternoon, while some were sleeping and others were trying to fall asleep, we heard a honk. We got up quickly and ran like rabbits, jumping across the forest to catch the big truck with red wooden bodywork and a white front, clearly used to move cattle judging from the manure on its floor.

We traveled around three hours on a paved road, grabbing onto anything, even each other, in our attempt to keep balance. Fortunately, we traveled without problems and were not stopped by Mexican authorities. After three hours, the truck slowed down and came to a full stop. Then, fast, it backed up into a grove.

As soon as we heard "Get off, quickly! Hurry!" we all jumped off the truck. Each of us was abandoned to their own luck, and we all ran to avoid being spotted. We kept opening paths in the forest, moving away from the road; until we came upon small houses made out of big Century plant leafs. We did not stop for fear that they may be inhabited or that we were going to be found there, and got deeper into that unknown grove of tall oaks.

Upon reaching a mountaintop covered with thorny bushes, from where we could see everywhere without being discovered, the guides decided that we should stay there for our safety. I was surprised when Norma asked me to sleep with her. I could not refuse, could I? I went to the place covered by leaves where she was. It seemed comfortable and inviting to sit under some thick bushes, while the others talked with the closest person in whispers.

I was very hungry, tired, sleepy and nervous, because it was my first time sleeping with a woman. The moonlight caught us by surprise, and apparently, Norma and I fell asleep happily, covered by the black plastic that my mom had packed in my bag, warming each other.

Following the instructions, we were respectful of women; those who wanted company, got it, and those who did not, were alone, but always close to somebody from the group spread out in that mountain, risking to be bitten by a snake, a scorpion or another poisonous creature.

Our sleep was interrupted by the scream of a man who arrived around eleven at night. "Come to eat!", he yelled. Without giving it a second thought, we got up with sleepy faces, stumbling on the tree trunks, and went to receive a piece of chicken, a tortilla and a soda pop. It was the most delicious chicken we ever tasted. Satisfied, after thanking him for the meal and wishing everybody a good night, we went back to sleep.

The following day reached us too quickly. We woke up at three in the morning, still feeling tired and sleepy. The journey had to continue. When we got up we realized that the plastic covering us was very wet, as if somebody had thrown a pale of water on it. Although it did not rain, the night dew dropped constantly from the trees. Without further delay –we did not have time even to go to the bathroom–, we started walking again towards some fields full of rocks under the moonlight.

Like chickens in a chicken coop

After walking for a while, we got closer to a place that seemed very busy for the street lights, but where nobody was awake yet. We were instructed to get on our fours to go by some houses without being seen and reached our next vehicle. This time it was a white trailer, 53 feet long and 18 wheels that seemed completely loaded with wood. That's the way the people traders had arranged to fool Mexican authorities. Underneath the trailer was a very narrow door through which the chubbiest guys from the group could barely pass.

We were getting in the trailer, looking around as if we had committed a very serious crime.

We were surrounded by dogs' barking everywhere, which increased the tension and the guides kept repeating, "Let's go, let's go, and hurry! Get in fast!".

When we were all locked in that tiny, dark and uncomfortable space, like chickens in a chicken coop, one of the guides began delivering instructions; "If you are still carrying alarm clocks, you need to turn them off. Nobody can say a single word. If somebody screams "Are you all OK?" you should not answer, unless you hear "green light" before the question, in which case you can answer because it is one of us asking".

The main rule was not to open our mouths at all; unless we heard the password, we could not talk even if the trailer was moving.

After the instructions, the guide gave us a bottle of water. I still remember, after so many years, the taste of that water mixed with the stuffy smell from being cooped up. We received also two thick bags for our bathroom needs during the trip. We were all equal there, with no differences of age, sex, or blood. We all suffered equally for our crime of being illegal, in our effort to find a better place and to help our families. I thought of my goals, my dreams and my family as a way to give me strength to keep going and get there.

With the strong engine roaring in the background, the trailer began moving slowly and gained speed gradually. In the darkness of that cage, we could only hear some people praying in low voice, the broken sound of the wind as we sped up, and the noise of the wood planks with each movement of the trailer.

We had not traveled long when Mexican authorities stopped us. We were panicked, being locked in there, just waiting for the moment they would discovered us and punished us for breaking the law. Luckily, they did not suspect anything and let us go.

Shortly after, we were stopped again, and with our hands between our legs, laying on the floor of the trailer, we listen attentively to the officials' and the driver's voices; we felt relieved when they let us go once again.

The third time we were stopped, we felt less worried because it was becoming a routine. As before, they let us go without suspecting anything.

In jail

It is strange that you sometimes risk your life to fulfill a dream; but everything has a limit and you choose your life over the so longed for dream.

The fourth time we were stopped at Palenque, Chiapas. We did not care anymore about the authorities, no matter how harsh they could be. We were too concerned about the heat we were suffering from being locked in the trailer. We were all sweating and lacking oxygen, but nobody said a word, as we were told. If somebody wanted to scream, nobody did it or they would have given away the whole group. But, when one officer got on top of the trailer to move away some of the planks, we could see the sun light, around three in the afternoon, and it was clear that we were caught. Then, many started yelling "Get us out of here!! We can't breathe! Please, get us out!" The officers immediately took the driver under arrest.

Accepting our fate, but happy to be able to breathe clean air. We got out of the trailer. It was amazing that although we feared the authorities, we were partially glad that they had caught us, since we had no idea how long we were going to be carried in that cage, risking death from asphyxia.

There are terrible situations in the stories of illegal immigrants. In some cases, the drivers abandon the trucks for unknown reasons, leaving them locked from the outside. In other cases, they travel for a long time in those cages and die of asphyxia; there are also many accidents. It is horrifying to think that you are there and that you can witness such awful events, and perhaps you won't even survive to tell the story.

Upon leaving that hell, without being mistreated by the authorities, we got onto a small bus with bars on the windows. The bus was very crowded and there was no space for all of us; the windows were shut and the sun was very hot. I felt sad and angry and I began feeling a tingling in my hands while the bus was driving us to jail. The tingling became a cramp extending to my arms, chest and face. My companions told me that when I got off I looked green, as if I were dying, with my hands and arms stuck to my chest, unable to move them. I remember that everything looked dark; in the prison's office, I fell to the floor as we were being taken in and couldn't move. I did not pass out; I was very conscious, but weak, unable to move my arms or legs, covered by a cold sweat and with tears in my eyes. I could also feel a lump in my throat.

Although they saw me sick, nobody stopped to help me; they just watched me fall. My fellow travelers could not help me because the authorities were in charge. Once everyone else was put in jail, a guard came over to rub alcohol over my arms and face until I felt better. Then, they locked me in immediately.

I still have in my mind the image of that tiny room. It was completely closed, with four walls, a small access behind bars to the office, a hole in the ceiling, a bathroom with a broken toilet in the open, green paint and some tires on the floor to sit down on. We had not taken a bath in several days and we smelled terribly; the more time we spent there, the worse it got.

Sadness filled everybody's eyes. Nobody said a word. We simply looked at each other faces while some of us cried noiselessly. Heartbroken and with the morale very low, some of my fellow travelers began taking a shower, naked, right there in front of everybody. Although showering seemed a good idea to get rid of the dirt and sweat, the smell became more intense after it, and we could do nothing to avoid it.

It is strange. When you are innocent, you wonder how life in prison would be —sometime ago; I myself had wondered how it would be to be in jail when I heard on the news that somebody was sentenced to five years for some crime. I laugh now remembering such naïve thoughts. When I was actually in prison, I did not want to even think about staying there. It was hell! The place smelled like a dead vulture. We were heartbroken and hungry; María and Norma brought us a sandwich in the afternoon, and that was the only thing we had to eat; thank you girls, wherever you are.

Women were not locked in like us. They were left in some open rooms that communicated with the offices. They could send the guards to the store to buy food as long as they tipped them good.

At night it was impossible to rest because of the heat of our bodies. If we tried to sleep, we had to do it sitting up because we did not fit in the room lying down. When the number of guards diminished, we started planning an escape from there, ready to risk everything. We realized that we could use a five-gallon bucket that was in the bathroom to step on it, reach the hole in the ceiling, stick our faces out and breathe fresh air. Shortly after we were enjoying the delicious air, many others realized what we were doing and we decided to take turns and forgot completely about our busting out effort.

We spent the night in line waiting for our turn to stick out our faces through the hole and breathe. While we waited, we talked about women, the trip, and many other topics as a way to forget where we were. Somebody had the great idea of asking "What do you think they will do with us?" Nobody answered; we could only feel the tension and hear the deep breathing of the guy who was enjoying his turn through the hole in the ceiling.

The following day, as soon as we heard the guards moving around the office, some of the guys began yelling, "When are you getting us out of here? We are hungry!" They even yelled some insults to the guards. A guard then approached the cell; he walked very calmly, showing off his authority. With a half smile and a deep soap-opera voice, he replied: "The worse you behave, the longer you will be caged." Upon hearing this, the guys yelling shut up instantly, like scolded children.

We knew that we were neither the first nor the last to be in that situation. We could see an infinite number of written names of past detainees on the walls. We passed time reading the graffiti; others wrote their own.

Without giving us even a glass of water, they proceeded to move us out twenty-four hours later, to board a bus that was going to take us back to the Guatemalan border.

Deported to Guatemala

On the way back, from Palenque to La Mezilla, all were silent in the bus. Some took advantage of the comfortable bus seats to sleep, while others, like me, were looking through the window to the mountains, Mexican towns and people at the side of the road. They did not seem different to me; they looked just like us. They were people struggling to take better care of their families, just like us, with the only difference that they were born on the other side of the border.

After traveling for six hours, we arrived to the Guatemalan border without a clear plan or strategy; we only cared about eating and sleeping. We felt free again, free in our country where we could move at our leisure, without being singled out or called "illegal aliens".

The instructions were to go back to the hotel where we had stayed before, and so we did. After taking a shower and eating something, we were so tired and sleepy that dropped dead until the following day.

The next morning I got up thinking of my family. I wanted them to know that we were safe. Byron accompanied me to look for a phone; we found it one mile and a half away. After waiting in line, I finally could call my sister in Jutiapa, Guatemala. She was very happy to hear my voice and promised to visit mom that same day to give her the news. Although being deported was not precisely good news, my mother felt very happy when she found out that, after almost two weeks,

I was well and thinking of them. We did not talk more than a couple of minutes, but we felt satisfied with the conversation.

We got lost a couple of times before boarding a small bus that took us back to the hotel. There we were surprised by the news that in any minute a cargo truck was coming to pick us up and try the crossing again.

Second attempt

That same afternoon, an old and rusty truck appeared; the driver was a tall man, wearing a hat and with a big mustache. We boarded it quickly. The truck had all its sides closed and we were only able to see the sky. We traveled for four hours not knowing where we were going. We were eager to move ahead and confident that this time we would succeed.

The truck came to a full stop. We crossed by running through a little village and entered a grove. There a black bull was waiting for us, with his bloody eyes and big horns. The bull was running along the corral and made us feel more frightened and we ran faster. Although the bull was inside the fence, we panicked thinking that it could jump over it and hurt us.

The guys were messing with the women afterwards who were running behind must of the time but when they saw the bull, they started screaming and overtook the group running, opening path through the thicket.

We were sweaty and still laughing when the night's cloak covered us. We decided to rest and eat something from our supplies; we would resume walking later, to reach the ronda-view point for the next vehicle to transport us.

Around eleven at night, we were lying among leaves, without knowing where we were, in the middle of nowhere. We could only hear the crickets' chirping and an owl moving close by.

The next event happened while I was half asleep. We were leaving and I was about to be left behind for oversleeping. The noise of people jumping onto the next cargo truck woke me up and I ran to join them. We traveled on that truck for not more than an hour. Then we got off again to keep walking and go around an immigration booth. We didn't know what time it was; we only knew that we were all doing well and the trip continued.

A Salvadoran coyote gives up

Walking, crawling and running like fugitives, we crossed wire fences, forests, fields, and even highways. We tried not to be seen by cars driving by in the dark night. Finally, we arrived to the place where we would be picked up by other transportation.

The sunlight came upon us waiting for the next vehicle. We saw then a Salvadoran guide leading a group of people from his country and Honduras who was walking all over the place, despairing. The guide was having a disagreement with his group; finally he decided to go back to his country and whoever wanted could follow him.

That group had suffered much more than we had. They came from farther away than us, had paid much more money than the Guatemalans and had crossed a couple of countries illegally already. The coyote did not care about the ones who wanted to continue. He was just tired and gave up. He wanted to go back and some followed him, including some Guatemalans.

The ones who lacked strength and faith left, and the strong, courageous and hopeful ones remained sitting down, watching the others go away to abandon their dreams. The deserters were throwing away the time and money invested in the adventure right there, in that field. They disappeared among the trees and never turned back.

Persevere and you'll succeed. At eleven thirty in the morning, a guide came over with sodas and cookies, followed by the old truck. This time the truck took us to a house surrounded by a wall of concrete blocks, where we were amazed to find the trailer, the same one in which we had been caught and deported in Palenque, Chiapas. The sight filled our hearts with bad memories. The trailer's owner cut a deal with the authorities and got the trailer back.

There we stayed parked two long days, inside a room with the door locked and without seeing the sunlight. The only moment I took with me from that place is a women's fight over food during a dinner and the long conversations we shared about our adventures.

A Salvadoran girl passes out

At three forty five in the morning of the second day, we were asked to board the "bad-luck trailer". Feeling very eager and hopeful, we rushed to get locked inside it once again, but this time we warned the guides that if we would suffer again from lack of oxygen, we would throw some of the wood boards onto the road to get out.

We reached Mexican land shortly afterwards. We did not know exactly where we were because we were always traveling during the night. During the day, we had to be crouched down and we could only see the shapes of the other people in the trailblazer.

Panic broke out when, after several hours, some people were unable to restrain any longer and started to relieve themselves. I remember a lady from Ecuador, who was sitting right next to me, who cut up a plastic gallon container and she relieved herself there, in front of me. The scene was very crude and intense. Although they defecated in bags, empty bottles and some other containers, the smell concentrated in that box with wheels.

Nobody said anything, because we had gone through too many things to ruin the trip just because of the nauseating smell of excrement and sweat. But, then a girl about 22 years old from El Salvador passed out. She fell to the floor and had seizures, kicking and throwing her hands around. Three fellow travelers helped her. They held her so she wouldn't hurt herself and fanned her with a hat. Our hearts were beating fast; we all felt unable to do anything for her. Then somebody yelled, "Open the door underneath to let oxygen in!" Immediately, the guys that were helping her opened the door and she finally quieted down.

Saving somebody's life is one of those moments that reveal our humanity and erase all personal interests. Luckily, the girl felt better after breathing some fresh air; we did too, satisfying our lungs with deep breaths of the outside air.

Along the trip, we were stopped infinite times by Mexican authorities. We followed the instructions we were given the first time, in the same trailer. The shrewd Mexican law officers yelled, "Do you want to stop and get something to eat? Mario, I need you to get out!" or other things like that, trying to check if it really was a load of planks. Luckily, nobody answered them, and no officer ever found us.

Mexico City

We traveled at least forty eight hours, caged in the dark, just drinking water until the trailer finally parked. Then we heard the password from the coyotes –they traveled in the front cabin with the driver– who asked us to open the door and get out immediately.

We descended as fast as we could. As we were coming out, we were getting on to a first-class bus, parked next to the trailer. There we were informed that the brilliant light glowing in the distance was the Federal District, Mexico City. We had left behind the biggest dangers, patrols, and difficult-to-cross towns. It was said that if you are in Mexico City, you are almost at the US border.

We could feel each other's joy; we shared smiles and shook hands. We were weak, sweaty and had dirty faces, but we certainly were happy.

The bus had curtains on the windows that prevented us from looking outside, but we could see through the front windshield the many patrol officers that let us go by while stopping other cars. We could also see some beautiful houses and lights everywhere. After one hour, we arrived to the Federal District's downtown area.

The bus was parked in a dark alley. Suddenly the guide yelled "Everybody out, quick! Duck and run to the white house, behind the bus! The door is open!" We flied out, like a swarm of bees, and entered the house.

There we said goodbye to our Central American brothers from the other groups. The following day when they brought a bicycle that was pulling a cart with seats which is called a tricycle in Mexico. The only ones remaining were the members of the original group from Guatemala.

We traveled a few blocks by tricycle and arrived to a house with the gate closed. We were received there by a Mexican, to whom the guys gave immediately the nickname of *Chupacabras* because he was ugly, thin and hairy. The Mexican was a really nice man and treated us kindly during our stay in the house.

We had been living two days already with Chupacabras when the guide asked us for another 500 USD each to continue the trip. They had run out of money. At once, I called my brother Samuel, who sent me the money as fast as he could. I also asked him to tell our mom that I was doing well and on my way.

In the house, there lived two girls of eight and ten years of age and an eleven-year-old boy. I had fun with them, helping them with their homework and learning myself. I learned, for instance, the Mexican National Anthem and to talk like them. (With a Mexican accent.)

Corrupt policemen

After a wait of six days in Mexico City, in a sunny afternoon with fresh breeze, the guide went to make a phone call. Later, he came back with good news: we would leave that same day to the bus station where we would board a bus to Matamoros, Tamaulipas, on the border between Mexico and the United States.

We traveled until three in the morning to a bus station. There, we waited until three in the afternoon for another bus that would take us to the United States' border.

Our hands started sweating when the immigration patrol stopped us at a control post, on the way to Tamaulipas. We almost cried from fear when one of the officers asked the guide and Adolfo, a twenty-three-year-old Guatemalan guy and my friend Mike's cousin, to get off the bus. The fear made my legs tremble, while I watched and heard the officers ask for documents with photographs in their hands.

Since we were illegal, we did not carry any identification, and least of all Mexican documents. We could only fake the Mexican accent, which we learned from the Chupacabras' kids. We could say that we were from such and such Mexican region and pronounce some learned words

Fearful to be discovered or to make a mistake when talking, we decided to feign being asleep when the officer approached our row. Mike leaned back against the window and I leaned against him, as if we were completely asleep. In fact, according to Mike's account, he even pretended to be asleep with his mouth open to convince the immigration officer. When they got to our line, the officer asked for identification to everybody in the row, on the other side of the aisle. Then he repeated in loud and authoritative voice "Your identifications, please!" He not only raised his voice, but he also tried to wake me up slapping my shoulder and shaking me. I did not know what to do for I was terrified, with my heart in my mouth and my hopes vanishing. Then I got an idea, one of those ideas that come in a second: I licked my lips, pretending to wake up, and groaned like saying "Let me sleep." You wouldn't believe it, but the officer gave up and left the bus.

Years can go by and that memory will always make my heart beat fast, once and again. We could have been deported again to the Guatemalan border, after enduring so many struggles.. Luckily, it did not happen and we went on. However, we were missing something: Where were Adolfo and the guide?

While faking to be asleep, we could not see if they had returned or had been detained, but we were a group, the bus was on its way, and to avoid raising suspicions in the Mexican people traveling with us, we did not inquire or look for them. Accepting with resignation that once at the border any other coyote could cross us if we paid the money reserved for the guide in the United States, we felt that we had nothing to loose.

Upon arrival to the next station, we had time to get off the bus and stretch our legs while people were boarding and exited. There we found out that Adolfo and the guide were with us. They had acted well doing their impersonations of Mexicans, and the officers let them go. Doña Rosa told a story that made us laugh. Since she did not know what to do or say, she decided to peal an orange as quickly as she could. When the officer approached her to ask her identification, she gave a huge bite to the orange, so big that the juice ran down her cheeks. The officer, then, only smiled and followed to the next row.

Just before arriving to Matamoros, Tamaulipas, the bus parked in front of a vegetable garden, following the guide's orders. He stood up and instructed us to get off and hide in a half-torn down shack nearby the street.

After traveling in first class, we went back to our true condition: we were illegal. It got worse; after less than five minutes, a patrol car appeared and two cops with drawn guns yelled to us that we should not resist or they would fire, and that they were going to deport us back to our home countries.

We did not know what to do. We raised our hands and gave up. At that point, the guide had the idea of offering them money to let us go. The cops asked him, with no hesitation, for One thousand dollars. The guide accepted, of course, since he had no alternative and it had been much more expensive to take the group until that point.

To my surprise, we did not have to wait for the vehicle that was going to pick us up there, as the same cops took us to a house where we could wait for new instructions. On the way to the house, since I was the youngest, I had to ride lying on top and across the cops' legs. The guide rode in the front cabin of the police truck, talking with the officers and trying to arrange deals for future crossings. They reached an agreement, and the officers promised to take care of everything, even with other authorities.

When we arrived to the house, we found a young man who had fallen asleep waiting for his ride, and his guides had left him behind somewhere in the desert in Texas. This guy asked our guide to join our group and so he did.

We waited three long hours until they came to take us. We were happy because we believed that we were on our way to *The Promised Land*, but unfortunately, that was not the case. We simply moved to other house, still in Matamoros, and we had nothing to eat but eggs and beans twice a day.

The walls in this house resembled the ones in a jail. They were covered with names written by people from Nicaragua, Panama, Costa Rica and South America. The lady in charge of the house treated us well and called us "her sons". Men and women slept in the same room on the concrete floor, laying on a mat and covered by a sheet, and we all used the same bathroom.

The crossing of Río Bravo

Five days later, following new instructions, we left at midnight, hidden in a pick up truck, to cross the Río Grande. We traveled for an hour and a half. The truck left us at some distance from the river so we wouldn't be detected by the intelligent devices that the United States Immigration has everywhere.

We walked for half an hour and arrived to the shore of the Río Grande around two in the morning. We advanced crouching among thorny bushes and making no other sound except for the cracking of twigs under our feet and the occasional "Shush!". We could see the majestic river where the moon was glowing, the river was running calmly and as wide as no other river we had seen before.

The guide took off all his clothes and we imitated him, except for the women that kept their underwear on. We entered the waters one by one, after packing our clothes in bags to keep them dry. We crossed the river floating on old tire tubes and once on the other side, dressed back up quickly, without saying a word or making any noise. The night was freezing; we were trembling, cold and fearful, but we were finally in the United States Of America.

We started running, feeling high in adrenaline, away from Mexico and towards our most precious dream. Our hearts were pounding and our breathing was much accelerated. Suddenly, the intense glow of two flashlights appeared in front of us, coming out of some bushes ahead. We knew immediately what was going on and ran in all directions, without thinking where to or caring about getting lost; we only wanted to escape from the Immigration forces.

After running for a while, we lost our persecutors by hiding under some dead plants. They were only two and we were many, and they got confused when we scattered, unable to follow each of us. Ms. Rosa fell into a furrow left by a plough. One of the officers stepped on her back while running after us but did not see her. Doña Rosa's back hurt for several days after that. Nobody knew what was going to happen next or where the others were. We could only wait.

The noise of a helicopter could be heard at the distance. The chopper's strong searchlight illuminated the area, looking for us. A voice was heard screaming "Don't look up, because they have special equipment to spot your eyes!" We were crouching down, covering our heads with our arms, unable to see what was happening. We could only hear the chopper flying around and see the strong searchlight that more than once illuminated the bush under which I was hiding, making me feel like the most helpless creature being hunted by a ferocious wolf.

Half an hour later, the chopper left and silence reigned, but for the relaxing sound of the river waters and the frogs croaking. Suddenly, we heard the guide calling us. When we gathered, we heard the chopper again, and although we tried to hide on a field of dead hay, we did it as a group and they spotted us. The helicopter stopped in the air just above us. Suddenly we heard, "Everybody, get out! You are surrounded!" We couldn't do anything, and we came out walking like criminals, with our heads low and our hands raised, towards the Immigration patrol. We were arrested and interrogated about our nationality. We all said that we were Mexicans. The three patrol cars, escorted by the helicopter, took us immediately back to the border and released us on Mexican territory.

Lost in the US

Upon returning to the house in Matamoros around eleven in the morning, we realized that Mike and Ñoño were missing. They did not come until the evening; they showed up with muddy clothes because they had been hiding in a tunnel until ten in the morning, when they felt so hungry that they decided to walk up to the side of the road and to wait there until being deported. They walked for two hours, with the immigration patrol cars coming and going without stopping, even when they signaled them to stop. Finally, Ñoño stood in the middle of the road, forcing a patrol car to stop and take them back to the border. From there, they took a taxi to the house.

Mike and Ñoño confessed that it was one of the worst nights, inside the tunnel full of mud and insects, hearing wolves howling in the distance first and then closer and closer as time went by.

Suddenly, the wolves were in front of them; in the dark, they looked like dogs. When the wolves saw them all covered in mud, they got more scared than Mike and Ñoño and ran away terrified.

One thing was the most important: the guys were safe now. They went to take a shower. Later, we ate dinner, told jokes and laughed, feeling proud of having reached the United States. The day ended when we abandoned ourselves to sleep.

In the United States

On our second attempt to enter the US; the following day, once again in the afternoon, we left in a vehicle that delivered us to a ranch. There were about fifty people gathered from Central and South America, including a Cuban couple with whom we would try to cross later and walk around the check point.

When it began getting dark, we started to walk along a path, one after the other. We were more than sixty people and we looked like a religious procession. I asked myself "Are we going to go through being so many?" In silence and bending over, we arrived again to the shore of the majestic Río Grande. Immediately, we got naked like we did before, only now we had no bags to put the cloths or tubes to float on.

Luckily, we crossed through a shallow part of the river. Nevertheless, Carlitos, a Guatemalan man who was walking next to me, was already swallowing water because he was very short and was carrying his clothes above his head to keep them dry. I grabbed his clothes at once to free him, allowing him to swim to the other shore. The river was calm, but it was not as shallow as we thought; in fact, it was so deep that I had to walk on my tiptoes and with my neck stretched out to avoid drowning and keep the clothes dry at the same time.

The night was cold and dark, and despite my usual courage, I was trembling from head to toe as I remembered the terrible experience we lived through before. We got dressed quickly and continued the trip through the thicket. Although we wanted to be as silent as we could, it was not easy being as many as we were. Crawling and running, we reached a street and crossed it after we checked that no car was coming. We entered a plowed field that was extremely muddy due to the recent rain. However, that was nothing.

From time to time, a light panned across the field. The guides warned us that the light was an Immigration camera; we, then, ran one by one not to be spotted, while the light was turning.

The next obstacle was even more horrifying. We had to cross a marsh, about twenty-one feet wide, with colder water than the river, and covered by grass. When swayed by the wind, the grass whistled strongly over a background of frogs croaking. Under the risk of being bitten by some poisonous animal, with the mud up to our knees, the water up to our waist and moving the bushes out of our way, we crossed it without any problem.

The night's cloak covered us. We felt protected and threatened at the same time. Things got worse when we reached a crossroad. The guides did not know which one to follow. Finally they decided to go to the right, and after half an hour of walking, we realized that we had taken the wrong path.

We went back then to the starting point and followed the other road; that ended up being the right one. We got to a cabin at four in the morning and slept there for a while, fearing to be attacked by the wolves that howled outside.

The following day the patrol car's sirens woke us up. They were approaching at great speed. We got terribly scared because we thought they had followed our traces and found our hideout. Luckily, the cars did not stop at our place and kept going.

We waited the whole day, and we ate only once. Finally, three pickup trucks came to collect us. We laid down in the back of the trucks, side by side, our bodies stacked on top of each other, and we traveled like that through the state of Texas for four hours.

At nightfall, the trucks stopped and somebody yelled "Get off quickly and cross the wire fence!" We jumped off at once and crossed the fence, some crawling underneath, some
Leaping over it, and some in any way they could. We ran through a thicket, over thorns and logs, in the dark.

We crossed a road, and looking in the distance, we distinguished a patrol car with its lights and siren on. We ran as fast as we could through a clear field, but we could still be seen from the road. We ran farther then, to disappear from sight into a prickly thicket.

The desert

We walked over thorns that torn our pants once and again. The bushes got smaller and smaller as we advanced, until they disappeared completely, and we arrived at a place that was only sand and sky. Everywhere we looked we could see the intersection of sky and land and nothing else. We did not know which direction to take. I was breathless, as if everything had evaporated from the face of earth. I had seen the desert in movies before, but I never imagined that it could be so impressive. I was standing there, surrounded by emptiness, in that habitat of snakes, poisonous spiders and hungry wolves.

We walked and walked and seemed like we were always at the same spot. We could not notice any difference in the landscape, all sky and land. The ground was loose and slippery, keeping us from progressing rapidly. We walked for a total of six hours, following a Mexican coyote, until we saw a grove ahead of us. It seemed to be five minutes away, but it took us an hour to get there.

We had been walking for seven hours by then, without drinking a single drop of water. Dying of thirst and exhaustion, a small aircraft startled us. It was flying so low, over the grove where we were resting peacefully. We forgot at once the exhaustion and the thirst and tried to hide wherever we could. The aircraft flew away and got lost in the horizon.

We decided to keep walking, fearing the possibility that the aircraft had spotted us and was going to come back with help to catch us. Some of us could barely go any farther; we were thirsty and walked more and more slowly, with our legs weakening at each step. We approached another grove, and one of the Mexican guys remembered that nearby there was a well with a mechanical pump. Somebody added, "There is where emigration hides out!"

We agreed that for everybody's sake someone had to scout around. Everybody started talking at the same time, and they were saying things like "Who will go? Who is courageous enough to go? If I weren't a woman, I would go". Nobody volunteered until Francisco; a twenty-seven-year-old man from Guatemala stood up and defiantly said "I will go". But he could not go alone, so I stood up next to him and agreed to accompany him. Everybody cheered and wished us luck. We started out, following the Mexicans who knew the way and would show us the direction, but who would not come with us to the well. We walked for twenty minutes; there the Mexicans stayed hiding in some trees after giving us directions to reach the place.

We discovered with joy the monstrous machine, serene and calm, like a hero or a saint, in the middle of nowhere. We ran happily towards it, not caring at all if the *Migra* was hiding there. As we approached it, we could hear the water louder and louder coming from the tank and overflowing to the ground.

We started drinking at once until we were satisfied. We laughed and even kissed the pump. We rolled to the ground, looking up to the sky and thanking God for that water source in the middle of the desert. We forgot for a moment the rest of our troubles.

Sighing happily, we left the place after filling up several gallon jugs and we followed the same road –or so we thought– we came from.

It caught us by surprise to not find the Mexicans when we arrived at the place where they were hiding out. We thought then that we were going to be lost in the desert and started yelling at the top of our lungs. They heard us and yelled back; we found them and returned altogether to the group.

When the others realized that we were bringing such treasure, they thanked and congratulated us, and we even received hugs from a couple of girls.

Our animal instinct

Human beings resort to their animal instincts when survival is at stake. Priorities also change, depending on the situation. In our circumstances, we were not worried about the electric bill, the leak in the roof, the car or the neighbor's gossip; we cared only for a glass of water.

We kept walking right after calming our thirst. We crossed many wire fences that could only be crossed by climbing over them. Once, two ladies from Panama were at the top of the fence and tried to help each other, but they lost balance and fell to the other side like ripe avocados. Luckily, they did not hurt themselves because they fell on the sand.

While walking towards a grove where the guides chose to spend the rest of the night, we began to hear wolves' howl, accompanied by a sudden wind. We quickened our pace in the dark of the night, guiding ourselves by the white light reflected by the floor, until reaching the grove.

Once there, with very hot bodies and clothes soaked by sweat, we sat a few minutes and chose a place to sleep.

When the sun came up, I was rolled up like a cat, with my hands between my legs, and the deep cold woke me up. Shivering, with blue lips, I got closer to Norma and another lady who was sleeping next to her. Without saying anything, they grabbed my hand and pulled me down between them, as a chick under the hen's wings. There, I fell fast asleep once again.

We were so tired that we did not wake up until eleven in the morning, when the guide found us. He was bringing a ham sandwich with mayonnaise for each one of us, along with a gallon of water for the group. We had the most horrifying experience that day, when we realized that we had slept next to a pile of bones, of all sizes, and we couldn't tell if they belonged to animals or a human soul.

Immediately after eating, we continued our journey, following the Mexican guides, who were experts on that road. Coming out of the grove, we could appreciate the desert in daylight; the wind was blowing in all directions, creating dust devils with the sand everywhere and the sun was burning like fire. We walked for only one hour and stopped to rest.

Suddenly, we jumped up; shaking our clothes when realizing that we had sat on a nest of small ticks that had crawled all over our bodies in less than three minutes. The ticks were so many that those little, blood-thirsty crab-like insects covered the floor in all directions. We shook our clothes well and ran out of there, to keep going on our journey.

We walked all day long until eight at night through the desert and with no water. We saw herds of deer, packs of wolves and even a group of armadillos among the trees –some things that we have never seen before.

When we reached the side of the paved road we sat down and waited for our transportation. Thirty minutes later, we heard cars stopping. Fortunately, they were the cars that came to pick us up. In seconds, we piled up in the corresponding pick up truck, each group in one; we couldn't see out, rise or move at all.

The cars from afar looked slanted by the weight of about twenty people. We traveled like that, protected by the darkness, until ten thirty at night. Suddenly, we heard police cars' sirens and saw colored lights flashing everywhere. Following the order to pull over, the driver slowed down and before it came to a full stop, we jumped off the truck and ran out towards the thicket. We had to cross a fence, at the side of the road, one of whose wires scratched my right leg, leaving an indelible scar.

Feeling the hot blood flowing over my leg, I jumped over the wire fence and kept going; it looked like a race, because Ulises was running right next to me. We reached a field of thick bushes that seemed impenetrable. We entered as we could, crawling and protecting only our faces from the prickles. We were escaping from an officer that still followed us yelling, "Stop or I'll shoot you! Stop! Put your hands up!"

Telling the truth, we did not know if in fact they were going to shoot us, but our only purpose was to escape, and until we would hear the first shot, we would keep running. After crossing a bushy field, we found an area of plowed land through which we could race faster. We hit once again a wire fence that we jumped over like the others to fall in a thicket. We felt safe and hid among the trees.

A while later, we heard something that sounded like people walking very slowly; we got very alarmed, since we thought that we had been found. Luckily, it was a Mexican guide, who was coming with Menchú and Doña Rosa. We felt relieved to know that we had company and that a Mexican guide was still with us; otherwise, we would have been completely lost.

The guide decided to look around to make sure that nobody else was hiding in the bushes. He warned us before not to move from there. Mrs. Rosa broke into tears when she saw the guide walking away, saying that we had suffered for nothing; we were there abandoned to our fate; thinking the coyote had deserted us.

The guide came back not very long after and gave us the bad news: the rest of the group had been arrested. We kept walking because the authorities knew that we were still at large and they could search for us with dogs. We walked until four in the morning and we got to a group of houses, close to the road, around which there were large and thick vines. We laid down there for a while. Nothing could be heard, except the crowing of a rooster in the distance. We fell asleep very quickly. We hadn't eaten or had anything to drink for a long time, and our bodies were weak and needing sleep.

The following day, we got up at ten in the morning, thinking to find a way out of there. We could see an old cabin in the distance, next to the road. We decided that we would go there at dark, and find transportation to continue our trip. We did not do it immediately because first we had to pass by some houses to get to the place.

The trip started earlier when at eleven in the morning a big storm gave us the opportunity to run over there without being seen. We got really wet but we reached the cabin. Luckily, the coyote was legal in the United States and he could move around more freely. As soon as the rain stopped, he went out to make a phone call and bring supplies. He returned two hours later with news that at night a car was going to be left for us parked at the side of the road.

We spent all day looking out through the little holes on the old cabin's walls, watching the cars racing through, until the night.

We waited until ten and the car did not appear. The guide, then, had to go out again to see what was happening. He made a phone call and was informed that the car couldn't be brought that day, but that the following day we would find a small bus parked on the street next to the cabin. We didn't believe anything that the person dealing with the guide said. We received the news cautiously, but we could do nothing else.

Arriving at Houston, Texas

The following morning, at six o'clock, we got up to watch the street, waiting for the bus. Just as it was said, exactly at seven in the morning, two cars arrived. The driver got out from a small bus and left the engine running. He boarded the car that was behind the bus and raced off.

We flew out, like lightning, and boarded the small bus. The guide would be the driver. We took off towards Houston, Texas. Feeling triumphant, we watched the buildings, houses and blonde, white people driving by. Now we were sure that we had crossed into the United States successfully.

Now, the story takes a new direction. Before we got to Houston, there was a squad of about fifteen police and Immigration patrols who gave us the order to stop. The guide did not stop and they began to pursue us with sirens, lights and a loudspeaker that was yelling things to us in English. Finally, when we saw that they were overtaking us, the guide decided to stop, but right before doing so, he told us to jump out of the bus. Ulises and Doña Rosa were traveling next to the bus door, so they could escape faster. The rest of us were surrounded by the patrol cars right away.

A cop ran after Ulises and finally caught him. Ulises struggled to free himself and almost succeeded, but a big and strong man approached him, lifted him up and threw him inside the car, as if he were throwing a bag of dirt. Ulises fell on his face and cut his lower lip leaving him severely bleeding.

Despite her size, Mrs. Rosa ran very far, but there was no place to hide. The officers followed her and she kept slipping away even when she was surrounded. Finally, they arrested her; put her hands behind her back, handcuffed her and brought her to the car that later would take us all to jail.

We were in prison for the second time, paying for the crime of being born across the fence. There was no place to sit among the crowd of illegal people that had been locked in the days before. They asked only about our nationality and threw us in jail until we were deported back to Mexico, that same night, since we had said we were Mexican.

On the way back to Mexico, many people –a majority of young men between sixteen and twenty five years of age– felt free. Some sang, others cried, others talked to each other. The bus was a racket, with people standing in the aisles and looking for a way to escape. Some were even planning to turn the bus over, as soon it would stop, and then escape.

We were silent so they would not realize that we were actually from Central America. An immigration officer came to the window –that had bars and was locked so we wouldn't have access to the driver. The officer told us: "Don't worry. If you did not make it across today, you will try again tomorrow. I know you very well and I know you are not going back home." A voice came from behind, among laughs, and replied: I would like to catch you just a few feet into Mexican land! The officer smiled and just watched while some young guys lighted a marihuana cigarette and started sharing it among themselves.

Hearing the young guys laughing and joking, we arrived at the Mexican border. They made sure to cross us over and then left through the tourist entrance door. We were back at the starting point for the second time.

Like beggars

The shrewd coyote instructed us to break the group off into pairs and to wait sitting on the park benches. He promised to pick us up there in a taxi. Ulises and I went away together and sat, as we were told, on one of the park benches to wait.

We looked like beggars, drunkards from the corner or crazy bums; we smelled much worse than any of them –after a week without a bath and walking all day with the same clothes through thickets, deserts and mud.

To make our situation worse, as the day went on and the guide did not come, food sellers began to appear. We had spent two days without eating anything but we had no money; the only thing we could do was watch, like begging dogs, as people enjoyed their breakfasts close to us, with their cups of coffee and milk and warm bread.

Finally, I had an idea: "Let's beg for some money to eat!" I said; Ulises did not believe that I would dare to beg, and he suggested that I should do it first. If I succeeded, he would do the same. I responded to Ulises' challenge standing up decisively and saying: "I will teach you how it is done", as if I were an expert. I approached a tall, blonde young lady, in a purple dress, who was carrying a basket. "Good morning, lady", I said, "Forgive me for bothering you. I am an illegal immigrant. I tried twice to cross the border and they brought me back. I have no money and haven't eaten in two days." The lady hesitated looking at my appearance, but she was concerned and helpful and suggested to buy me something to eat instead of giving me money, because she was not sure I wanted the money to buy food. I accepted very happily and went with her to a stand where many things were sold. She asked me what I wanted, and I answered: "Whatever you want, anything." The good-hearted lady bought me two *pupusas (stuffed tortillas)*. I was very moved by her gesture and thanked her dearly and heartily, looking at her in the eyes; as I went back to where Ulises was waiting.

I would like to know today who that lady is to reward her as she deserves.

Thanks should be given to all who have offered a glass of water to the thirsty and food to the hungry, because we don't know when it will be our turn to be in that situation.

Encouraged by my success, Ulises stood up and walked around. He came back soon after with a few coins that we used to buy a soda pop. We could not believe what we had done, or the way we looked. At least, we could eat something and we only had to wait.

One hour later, a tall guy of dark complexion, wearing sunglasses, came over to us and ordered us to follow him. We did not know him and we could not ask him anything, because he turned quickly. We followed him, knowing that we had nothing to loose. Luckily, he was the taxi driver and took us back to the well-known house where we stayed before.

In the house, there were all the people that had been arrested before us, including our group and everybody else. We also found out that another trip to try crossing the border was scheduled for the following day.

Abandoned by the coyote

Our perseverance to get to our destination was leaving intense marks on our bodies, making them weaker and used to strange routines. As if we were doing something natural, we got naked in front of everybody to cross the river for the third time.

Once on the other side, we separated from the group and begged the coyotes not to make us walk like they did the last time. They were also tired and shared the feeling; this time we only walked for an hour and hid next to the street, lying on the ground, while the guides went to find some transportation.

We spent the night there, in the open, just like the other times, as if we were wandering animals, at the mercy of human's and nature's laws, sleeping under bushes and feeling the cold deep down in our bones.

The following day, one of the guides returned with a sandwich for each of us and a gallon of water for all. He told us that we were going to be picked up at night. We waited with our bodies hurting after sleeping on the hard floor and cold –it was winter. We could hear the sirens of the immigration patrol cars that were coming and going, yelling out orders to stop through their loudspeakers. All was a chaos that lasted the whole day. As if that weren't enough, we were in a grass field and we had to scare the cows that were coming over our way. We spent all day doing that until night fell.

As it was agreed upon, at nightfall we got closer to the street and minutes later a pickup truck was parked and left. We saw no other cars coming on the road, and after jumping over the wire fence, we all rapidly got in the truck, making the noise like a load of stones. We laid our bodies on the side, trying to make space for everybody, even if that meant to travel with the shoes or some other body part of a fellow traveler against our face.

The guide drove too fast, and minutes later, trying to turn in a sharp corner, we heard the squeak of the wheels that began smoking. This alarmed a patrol car that was following us from afar; it turned on the siren and lights and sped up to catch us.

We knew the routine well: the car stopped and we all ran out to look for refuge in the thicket. This time a voice through the loudspeaker from a patrol car parked behind the truck yelled: "Don't run! You can go, we are State patrol!"

Without believing them, we kept running like deer, down to a huge plowed field. We continued racing through it until we saw that the patrol car was leaving.

One of the guides returned to the truck to see if they had left the key –the driver was so smart that he ran out without taking the key with him. Unfortunately, the officers had taken it. One of the Mexicans knew a way to start the truck without the key, but he was fearful that he could be accused of stealing the truck and end up worse than before.

Disheartened, we had to leave the truck and walk. Finally, we arrived to one side of the freeway around four in the morning. We decided to stop and rest from what had happened and the hours of walk, right there next to some trees.

The following was a beautiful, sunny day with birds singing and flying around. Of course, there was also the noise of cars speeding down the freeway. Some people were stretching out, others were rubbing their eyes, others were yawning, but all had a winning smile, thanking God for being able to live one more day, thinking perhaps that this was going to be the last dawn we would contemplate. We were acting normally, pretending nothing was happening; sometimes we forgot where we were, and greeted each other in the morning as if we were a family.

At ten in the morning, two men appeared as if dropped from the sky; they brought supplies and water. We were surprised that they found us so quickly. The two men belonged to the same organization as the coyotes. The guides planned the route to follow in order to go around the Immigration control post that we couldn't get past before.

We got out without being seen and resumed our trip by foot. We hid in the bushes to avoid being spotted by the cars running down the freeway. Later, we went further into the desert, going through places similar to the places we walked through before. We even saw a black buffalo; it was very ugly, with big curvy horns. It was observing us attentively while we walked, as carefully as we could, avoiding sudden movements that could provoke it.

We stopped to rest around eight at night, in a place full of bushes with huge thorns and close to the street where we would be picked up later. We fell asleep. It was not until the following night that we heard the engine of the car coming for us. This time the story was completely different.

Action, suspense, and drama made up our experience this time on the road, and the story took a drastic and definitive turn. The guides' organization was not so organized after all; they did not know the appropriate time and place to attempt the crossing without being caught.

We traveled by car for two hours. When we were in the city of Corpus Christi, Texas, I felt a terrible cramp. I couldn't move because Ñoño's leg rested over my foot and was pressing against the metal of the car. To make my torture even worse, the least desirable thing happened: the police caught us once again. We didn't know it then but this was our last attempt and we eagerly jumped out of the car. One officer was already ahead of us, and he grabbed Byron and tried to handcuff him. Byron, feeling left behind, began fighting with the officer. In the struggle, he torn his shirt and broke a rosary that he wore around his neck which was a gift from a Salvadoran girlfriend. The officer scratched Byron's neck and chest, but he was able to free himself before more policemen arrived.

I could not run very quickly because the cramp in my foot prevented me from running normally. The racket gradually grew, particularly with the arrival of three more police cars, with their sirens and lights. The cars were left in the street while the cops were chasing us on foot.

Eating from a dumpster

We experienced our biggest defeat when the coyote –the person to whom we had paid and entrusted our lives– gave up and hopelessly kept saying: "If we get caught, let's say that we are from Guatemala, to be sent there." Some women broke into tears upon hearing vanquished expressions such as "I can't go any longer!" and insults thrown at the guide from the angry people who disagreed with him.

Many of us left home very determined to arrive to our destination or die in the attempt; that's why we could not agree with the guide and decided to keep going on. All this was taking place at the same time the officers, whose number was growing by the second, were chasing us through a big plowed field.

We were running against the wind and the law, holding hope and faith in our hands, getting away from the human hunters and towards our dream.

We kept walking through thickets and plains, with hearts pounding fast but very sure of our desire, restraining our feelings of despair for them not to betray us. Feeling a lump in our throats, we arrived at a ranch. There we tried to get some water from the faucets, but each one we opened only dispensed some kind of chemical or insecticide.

Heartbroken in that unknown world that did not speak our language, we could see far away a tenuous light. We had to walk two hours, sidestepping many obstacles. We endured one journey more, sustained by our faith, hopes and our families' prayers. This time we did not have a guide, a map or any sense of direction.

When we were close to the light, we hid in the bushes close to the street. We could see from there that the light belonged to a tobacco and liquor store. While discussing our next move we found out that Menchú held a permit to work in the United States because he had been there before; he was in Guatemala only for a family visit and was on his way back.

Menchú was already safe; furnished with a working permit, he could move around without problems. We discussed the next steps, sitting in a circle on the grass at four in the morning. Menchú was our only hope, and without the group suggesting anything –the group was composed of Doña Rosa, Ulises, Byron, Menchú and myself–, he volunteered to go out and call a relative to come and pick us up. His only condition was to be accompanied by one of us.

Although Menchú tried to play hero, problems arose. He invited Ulises to go out with him, since Ulises was tall and white. Ulises never refused, but he did not accept either; he remained undecided for several minutes. Noticing that Menchú was getting discouraged, I got up and volunteered to go with Menchú for the sake of the group. Menchú could speak some English, and therefore, he could help to get us out of such nightmare.

We had walked for no more than three minutes along the paved road when a patrol car stopped us.

They forced us to get inside the car and started interrogating us. They asked us if we were going around stealing cars, or if we were part of the group that had escaped the night before. We denied everything and said that we came from California. Even when they shined their flashlights on our muddy shoes; Menchú talked to them for a while in English and they let us go. We could not believe it.

We felt more confident and assured then, much less fearful knowing that we were already in the United States. Menchú made a call to his relatives in Los Angeles, California, from the payphone that was outside the store, on the other side of the road. From there we could still watch the police cars coming and going.

I decided to give Menchú some privacy and went to the back of the store. There was a dumpster. At once, I started looking for edible food and filling bottles with some of the drinks disposed in the trash. I took with me a box of strawberries, half of them rotten, and several bottles of soda, mixed with other remnants to share them with my fellows, since we did not have a single cent to buy any food.

We were about to return to our hideout, when a police car and an Immigration van parked right in front of us. Two officers got out at once, asking for our papers. Menchú took his wallet out and showed his papers, but I did not have any. I had to be detained. One of the Immigration officers grabbed my arm and told me, "You are coming with me."

I felt all alone and heartbroken for the first time on that journey. To make things even worse, the Immigration officer started doubting my nationality for he did not believe I was Mexican. The few things I learned from the Chupacabras' children in Mexico City. – I could sing the Mexican National Anthem and I did it to prove that I was Mexican– which saved me from being deported to Guatemala.

They had me inside the Immigration vehicle touring around, from one place to another, until they suddenly opened the door again and Adolfo and two Mexican guides were thrown inside. Adolfo and I were partially relieved to find each other; at least we weren't alone anymore.

We were deported the following day to the border and the guides left us in the park, while they made some arrangements. We stayed in the park, as they told us. We spent the time talking, under the disapproving looks of the passers-by to whom we must have seemed like street drug addicts. Suddenly, I thought of collect calling my aunt Juana, who was in the capital city of Guatemala, and asked her to tell my mother that I was doing well and about to cross the border.

One, two, three hours passed and the guides did not come. We were desperate and we thought of looking for a church or temple of any religion to ask for help. After walking for a while, we were convinced that the guides had abandoned us and arrived to a huge Catholic church. We did not find a priest anywhere inside; we only saw some churchgoers kneeling and praying.

We also kneeled and directed our prayers and cries for help to the Divine Creator. God heard us and answered us through a young woman who worked in one of the church offices and who fortunately gave us twenty Mexican pesos to go to the closest shelter where we could eat and sleep.

We left the church feeling very happy. When going by the park, we decided to wait a while longer for the guides. We knew now what we were going to do next and felt calmer. Sitting on the concrete benches in the park, we talked about the ungrateful guides who left us stranded even when they were aware that we did not have a place to go and we were hungry, dirty and penniless.

It was like a miracle when a coyote came for us. He had taken a shower and changed his clothes. He picked us up in a taxi and took us with him to the same house that at this point, —the fourth time—, felt like ours. We heartily thanked the guide and the owners of the house for letting us stay there.

By then, we did not have any news at all about Menchú's group or the Guatemalan coyote's group.

Disguised as North Americans

The following four days, we slept in an old car that was parked in the house's garage, because the rooms were occupied by other groups. Everyday, new groups of people were arriving and leaving.

When we told them our story, nobody wanted to take us with them to cross the border, superstitiously thinking that we would bring bad luck to them. The guides handed us over and disappeared, leaving us completely alone. We asked and begged to be taken with different groups, but all of them refused to do it.

Adolfo had an uncle in North Carolina, and decided to call him. Adolfo was nicely surprised to hear that his uncle would help us, and that, luckily, he had a friend in a place close to Matamoros. Adolfo then called his uncle's friend and he promised to help us.

During our stay in the garage, a good-hearted young man, Juan, bought us food. Juan worked for the owners of the house. I had to exchange my new shoes –I wore them for the first time the day I left home– for some old, worn-out ones to get some money to eat. Thank you, Juan.

On the fourth day, a tall, dark man, with a thick and black mustache, came to collect us. He drove a taxi and took us to the house in a place called El Progreso in the state of Tamaulipas, which belonged to a sixty-year old lady, with grey hair and wearing an apron. She treated us as if we were her own sons.

Two days later, there appeared a Texan man, wearing boots and a hat. He had been hired by Adolfo's uncle to cross us, but this time through a different place. He told us the news that somebody would come that afternoon to take us.

Encouraged by the news, we waited very eagerly all through the afternoon. At nightfall, two boys, thirteen- and seventeen-years-old, arrived and told us to follow them; anxious to start this new adventure, we walked for less than ten minutes and reached the river.

The boys informed us that the neighborhood was next to the Río Grande, and since there were scarce Immigration officers guarding the place, it was very easy to cross without being caught.

Once at the river, we got off our clothes, put them in a bag and swam quickly to the other side. There we got dressed and started walking at a fast pace, crossing a wire fence and a field. To our surprise, the Texan's house was about two miles from the river, and in less than half an hour we were safe and sound in a house of the United States of America. Everything was so easy that it seemed a dream. It was amazing and unbelievable having crossed that way, with two young boys as guides, after suffering so much during the times before when we were in the hands of big organizations.

When we told our story to the Texans, they were surprised by hearing everything we had gone through. They consoled us and told us that they would cross us by the dividing line, right in front of the Immigration post and we would not have to walk much. We were practically there. Although we were already on the other side, we still had to pass the checkpoint, the same that we had tried to avoid so many times taking a detour through the desert.

The following day they bought us very nice cowboy's clothes and new shoes. We felt that we had reached our goal, because were eating well and already living on the other side.

We were very worried about having to cross under the authorities' noses.

The second day, they decided to take Adolfo first. They couldn't take many people at once, because they were going to use their children's birth certificates as the documents to identify us. They would go with their other young children to make it look like a family trip.

I spent the whole day chewing my fingernails, waiting for news about Adolfo and alone in the house. I was desperate and thought that I was left stranded there. Although I had a roof over my head, I wasn't happy because that was not my goal. Finally, I fell asleep on the sofa in their living room.

The following morning, thinking that I was alone, I went out to see the dawn and found, to my surprise, that the cars of the Texans were in the driveway. They had already come back. When they got up, they gave me the great news: Adolfo was crossed without any problem and now it was my turn.

That same day, after I took a good shower and smelled nice, we set out for the trip towards my future. We got to the Immigration control post in less than an hour. There, we were asked if we were all American Citizens; The driver talked to the Immigration officers the whole time while I played with the kids in the back of the car. We were asked to get off for them to have search dogs sweep the car and were asked to show our documents while asking us about our destination. Finally they let us go wishing us a good trip.

Arriving at our destination

WOW! We never, ever thought that our heroic deed could be so easy. I felt accomplished, very lucky and alive. I knew that we could have died in the attempt, but our perseverance, our families and our friends made it possible to be there, very close to our goal, with victory in our hands and a triumphant smile at the end. Half an hour after passing the Immigration checkpoint, we picked up Adolfo at a hotel where he had spent the night before, and went on to North Carolina, to his uncle's house.

We drove without stopping until Houston, then on to Atlanta, South Carolina, and from there to North Carolina. Adolfo's family welcomed us enthusiastically, with hugs and smiles. I was introduced to the family; they were friendly and loving people who treated me like another family member. They paid the Texans for the trip, and I promised them that my brothers would send them the money later for the fee the Texans charged to bring me.

We spent the afternoon celebrating Adolfo's success, since he had already accomplished his goal. We did not know anything about the others; on the other hand, I had still some way to go until reaching my destination, but they told me that I was safe there.

During the following three days, Adolfo's uncle, a very nice man, tried to find me a job in different places, but nobody wanted to hire me because I was only seventeen. The third day, I received the money from my brothers, and I could repay Adolfo's uncle and buy a bus ticket to Kentucky, my final destination.

That same afternoon I left for North Carolina in a very comfortable bus. I knew that very soon I would be with my loved ones, and I was very anxious to see my brother. At night, the cities were full of lights and activity. I was getting farther and farther from my homeland, but I felt hopeful of finding a better future and being able to reward my parents, as I promised.

Finally, we arrived in Kentucky. I noticed that my brother was looking at me through the glass wall in the station's waiting room. I was so moved that I hurried up and couldn't find the exit. Once I was in front of my brother, we hugged each other for several seconds, without saying a word. That was my brother's way to welcome me. We went then to look for my five-year old niece who was playing video games. When she saw me with Arnoldo, she ran into my arms crying "He's here! He's here!"

We picked up my sister-in-law from work and went to their home. We talked there about our family and my trip. They showed me my room that Isabel, my sister-in-law, had prepared especially for me a long time ago.

Dream Accomplished

At night, I hugged the sheets thanking God for giving me the strength and faith that kept me alive. I could not fall asleep. I remember that I observed once and again the walls of the room under the weak light that was coming through the window. I wondered if I was dreaming or in fact I was really there, living my precious dream.

I wish all the luck in the world to the other adventurers who shared my trip and remember; you can get to the United States legally, without risking your life.

After a few days I started working in a drum facility making $5 an hour on 12 hours days and 8 hours on Saturday; I was determined to help myself & my family. I am proud to say that I did and keep doing it. But if I had known what the road was going to be like; I would have taken a different route.

The start (end)

Wait! If you are wondering what happened to the other people, I found out later that Menchú had succeeded in his attempt and they got to their destination. Amazingly, the Guatemalan guide's group did not get caught and finally arrived to the United States with the help of a rancher and a Texan lady.

Feliciano Marroquín Orantes - 2007

ÍNDICE

Dedication	5
Prologue	7
Origins of the story	9
The Farewell	11
Leaving the nest	15
The Instructions	17
Unknown roads	19
The Hotel	21
Threatened with shotguns	23
A horrifying experience	25
Crossing the Mexican border	27
Like chickens in a chicken coop	31
In jail	33

Deported to Guatemala	37
Second attempt	39
A Salvadoran coyote gives up	41
A Salvadoran girl passes out	43
Mexico City	45
Corrupt policemen	49
The crossing of Río Bravo	53
Lost in the US	55
In the United States	57
The desert	61
Our animal instinct	65
Arriving at Houston, Texas	69
Like beggars	71
Abandoned by the coyote	73
Eating from a dumpster	77
Disguised as North Americans	83
Arriving at our destination	87
Dream accomplished	89
The start (end)	91

Editorial LibrosEnRed

LibrosEnRed es la Editorial Digital más completa en idioma español. Desde junio de 2000 trabajamos en la edición y venta de libros digitales e impresos bajo demanda.

Nuestra misión es facilitar a todos los autores la **edición** de sus obras y ofrecer a los lectores acceso rápido y económico a libros de todo tipo.

Editamos novelas, cuentos, poesías, tesis, investigaciones, manuales, monografías y toda variedad de contenidos. Brindamos la posibilidad de **comercializar** las obras desde Internet para millones de potenciales lectores. De este modo, intentamos fortalecer la difusión de los autores que escriben en español.

Nuestro sistema de atribución de regalías permite que los autores **obtengan una ganancia 300% o 400% mayor** a la que reciben en el circuito tradicional.

Ingrese a www.librosenred.com y conozca nuestro catálogo, compuesto por cientos de títulos clásicos y de autores contemporáneos.

www.ingramcontent.com/pod-product-compliance
Lightning Source LLC
Chambersburg PA
CBHW021003230426
43666CB00005B/260